WORLD OF BELIEFS

WITHDRAWN

In the same series:
- ○ Judaism
- ○ Christianity
- ○ Islam

First published in the United States in 2002
by Peter Bedricks Books, an imprint of
McGrawHill Children's Publishing
8787 Orion Place
Columbus, OH 43240
www.MHkids.com

**McGraw-Hill
Children's Publishing**
A Division of The **McGraw·Hill** Companies

ISBN 0-87226-685-0

Buddhism
was created and produced by McRae Books
via de' Rustici, 5 – Florence (Italy)
info@mcraebooks.com

SERIES EDITOR Anne McRae
TEXT Anita Ganeri
ILLUSTRATIONS Studio Stalio (Alessandro Cantucci, Fabiano Fabbrucci,
Andrea Morandi), Paola Ravaglia, Gian Paolo Faleschini
GRAPHIC DESIGN Marco Nardi
LAYOUT Laura Ottina, Adriano Nardi
REPRO Litocolor, Florence
PICTURE RESEARCH Elzbieta Gontarska
Printed and bound in Italy by Nuova G.E.P., Cremona

WORLD OF BELIEFS

Anita Ganeri

BUDDHISM

PETER BEDRICK BOOKS

TABLE OF CONTENTS

Note – This book shows dates as related to the conventional beginning of our era, or the year 0, understood as the year of Christ's birth. All events dating before this year are listed as BCE, or Before Current Era (ex. 928 BCE). Events dating after the year 0 are defined as CE, or Current Era (ex. 24 CE), wherever confusion might arise.

What is Buddhism?   8

The Buddha's Youth   10

The Search for
        Enlightenment   12

The Teachings   14

After the Enlightenment   16

Monks and the Monastic Life 18

Buddhism Splits and Spreads   20

Buddhist Texts   22

Buddhism in Sri Lanka   24

Buddha Images and Stupas   26

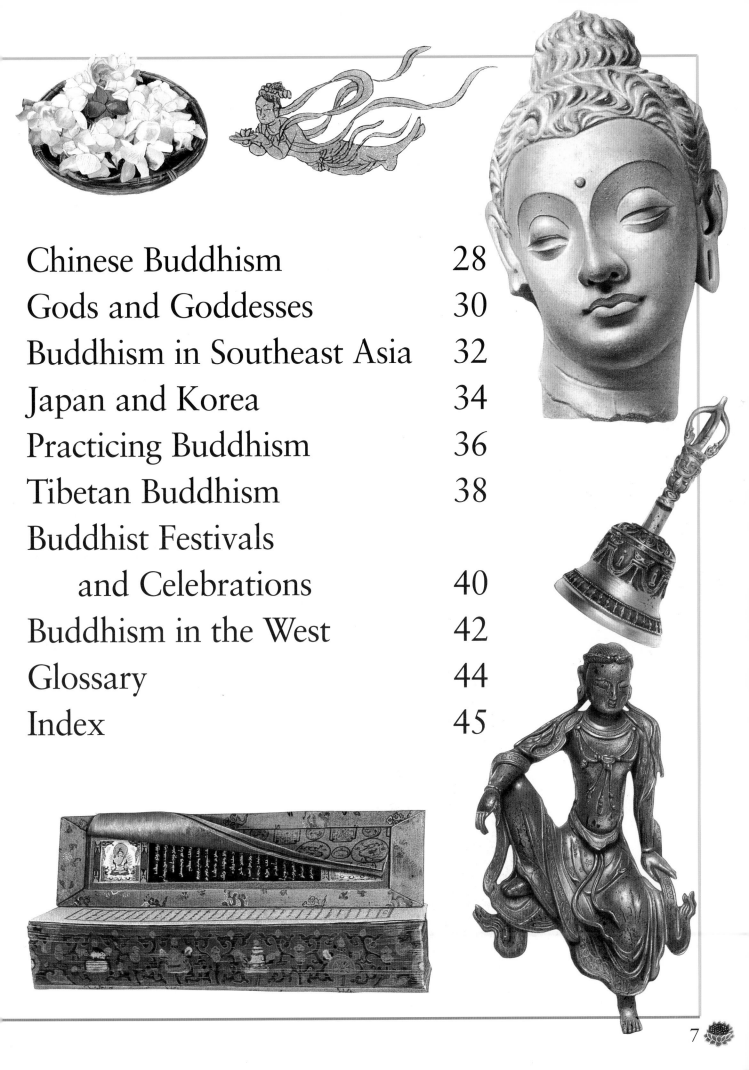

Chinese Buddhism 28

Gods and Goddesses 30

Buddhism in Southeast Asia 32

Japan and Korea 34

Practicing Buddhism 36

Tibetan Buddhism 38

Buddhist Festivals
  and Celebrations 40

Buddhism in the West 42

Glossary 44

Index 45

What is Buddhism?

Buddhism began in northern India about 2,500 years ago. Its founder was a royal prince called Siddhartha Gautauma who became known as the Buddha. Siddhartha was brought up to be a king, protected from the sadness of the outside world. When he finally saw suffering, it changed his life. He left his palace behind and set out to discover why people suffered and how suffering could be stopped. He became enlightened, which meant that he realized the truth about life. Then he spent the rest of his life teaching people what he had learned. Buddhists follow the Buddha's teachings as a guide for their lives.

This is a Tibetan lama. Lama is the Tibetan word for a spiritual teacher or leader. Lamas are usually monks.

Buddhist teachings

The Buddha's teachings are called the dharma. The Buddha taught that each person must realize the truth of life for him or herself. His teachings were only meant as a guide or a path to follow.

This eight-spoked wheel is a symbol of the Noble Eightfold Path, a key part of the Buddha's teaching (see page 14).

Monks and nuns

After his **enlightenment**, the Buddha lived as a monk. He traveled around India, teaching the dharma. Some Buddhists follow his example and become monks or nuns. Together they are known as the **sangha**. Monks and nuns live very simple lives, dedicated to studying and teaching the dharma.

Lotus symbol

For Buddhists, lotus flowers are powerful symbols. Lotuses grow in water, with their roots in the mud. But the flowers rise above the mud to bloom on the surface. In the same way, people can rise above life's sufferings to achieve enlightenment.

Lotuses also symbolize the Buddha's beauty and goodness.

Places of worship

Many Buddhist monks live in monasteries or temples called **viharas**. These are also places which ordinary Buddhists visit to honor the Buddha and pay their respects to the monks. This temple in Thailand is beautifully designed and decorated to inspire the people who visit it.

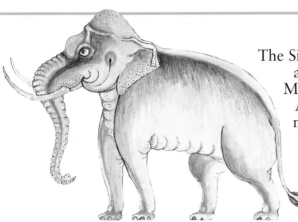

How Buddhism spread

The Silk Road was a series of trade routes across central Asia which linked the Mediterranean with India and China. Along the Silk Road, people carried new ideas, as well as goods to trade. Buddhism spread from India into China along the Silk Road. Chinese Buddhists also traveled to India to learn more about their faith.

Sacred elephant

According to legend, Queen Maya, the Buddha's mother dreamed that a white elephant entered her side. The elephant was an omen and ten months later, Siddhartha was born. In ancient India, white elephants were very precious. They belonged to the king and were said to guarantee the kingdom's prosperity.

Buddhist pilgrims faced a perilous journey across barren deserts and high mountains where bandits and wild animals lay in wait.

The demon in the center of the amulet has glaring eyes and sharp tusks. It was created by the Hindu god, Shiva.

Other influences

In some places, Buddhism has mixed and mingled with the religion that was there before. These influences are often shown in local art and architecture. This Tibetan lucky amulet (left) is adapted from a Hindu symbol. It is said to protect the wearer from evil demons.

Around the world

From India, Buddhism spread to the neighboring countries and beyond. Today, there are about 400 million Buddhists. Most still live in Asia where Buddhism began. More recently, since the early 20th century, Buddhism has also become very popular in the US and Europe.

This figure of the Buddha on a turquoise throne comes from China. Buddhism spread to China in about CE 100.

Future Buddha

Buddhists believe that the next Buddha will be Maitreya (shown below). At present, he lives in a heavenly realm called the Tusita Heaven, waiting for Buddhism to decline in thousands of years' time. Then he will appear on Earth and teach people how to live.

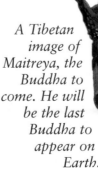

A Tibetan image of Maitreya, the Buddha to come. He will be the last Buddha to appear on Earth.

The Buddha's Youth

According to tradition, the Buddha was born in about 563 BCE into the royal family of the Shakyas. His father ruled a small kingdom in the foothills of the towering Himalayan mountains (in present-day Nepal). He was given the name Siddhartha and the family name Gautama. He also became known as Shakyamuni, "the sage of the Shakyas." Many marvelous legends surround Siddhartha's birth and youth. These were recorded centuries after his death and may not be historically exact.

Nevertheless, they provide a wonderful insight into the beginnings of the Buddhist faith.

The Buddha's birth
Siddhartha was the son of King Suddhodana and Queen Maya. Shortly after his birth, a wise man, called Sita, visited the king's palace. From special marks on the baby's body, he saw that Siddhartha would become the **Buddha**.

Previous lives
The Buddha lived many different lives before he was born as Siddhartha Gautama. The stories of these lives are told in a collection of tales called the Jatakas. In many of these, the Buddha appears as an animal on his way to enlightenment.

This painting from Thailand shows the Buddha in one of his past lives. As he made his way through the forest with water for his parents, he was shot with a poisoned arrow by a Benares king. By acts of great faith, he was brought back to life.

Soon after his birth, the Buddha raised his right arm and proclaimed, "I will be he who walks before all laws that have merit at their root."

The four sights
Siddhartha led a very sheltered life in his father's luxurious palace. His father made sure that he knew nothing of poverty, suffering, or death. One day, Siddhartha left the palace. He saw an old man, a sick man, a dead man and, finally, a holy man. The experience changed his life.

Siddhartha sees illness for the first time.

As Siddhartha stole away from the royal palace, under cover of darkness, the gods appeared and held up the horse's hooves with their hands so that no one would hear him leave.

Leaving home

Siddhartha decided to spend the rest of his life searching for the truth and a way out of suffering. That night, he left the palace and his wife and newborn son behind. He cut his hair and exchanged his fine clothes for a monk's simple robes.

Ancient India

The 6th century BCE, when Siddhartha was born, was a time of great spiritual activity in many parts of the world. In India, people had started asking questions about the order of the world and human destiny many centuries before.

The map shows the two most important cities of the Indus Valley Civilization and Siddhartha's birthplace of Lumbini.

In about 2,500 BCE, a great civilization thrived in the Indus Valley in northern India. These stone seals come from the ancient city of Mohenjo Daro.

The Hindu god Shiva.

The Hindu elephant god Ganesh is the son of Shiva and his wife, Parvati.

Hinduism

The Hindu religion began in India about 4,000 years ago. It grew out of a mingling of ideas from the Indus Valley religion and that of a people called the Aryans.

11

The Search for Enlightenment

Siddhartha spent many years traveling through northern India. He lived as a homeless monk, eating only the food he could beg. He tried different ways of finding the truth but none of them worked. Finally, he made his way to a river and sat down to meditate under a sacred tree. During the night, Mara, the powerful god of evil, tried to force Siddhartha to give up his search. For, if Siddhartha discovered an end to suffering, Mara's powers would be destroyed. But Siddhartha defeated Mara and finally saw the truth about life. From then on, he became the Buddha, the "enlightened one."

Siddhartha ate so little that he looked like a skeleton.

Going without

After leaving home, Siddhartha became a disciple of several great teachers of meditation. But he did not find the answers he sought. For six years, he lived in the forest with a group of holy men. Their way of life was very hard. Siddhartha wore filthy, coarse clothes that made his skin sore. In summer, he sat in the burning sun. In winter, he bathed in icy water. He ate so little that he fainted with hunger.

*Below: Siddhartha accepts a bowl of rice before he begins his night of **meditation**.*

The Middle Path

After his dream about Indra, Siddhartha changed his way of life and left the forest behind. The idea of the "Middle Path" is very important in Buddhism. Later, the Buddha taught his followers that happiness does not come from great luxury or great hardship. People should follow a Middle Path between these two extremes.

Left: Legend says that the god Indra, playing the lute, appeared to Siddhartha in a dream. He told him to avoid excess and follow the Middle Path.

The struggle with Mara

As Siddhartha sat under the sacred tree, he was attacked by Mara, the evil one. Mara summoned up a dreadful storm, strong enough to turn whole towns to dust. Then he sent an army of terrible demons who hurled rocks and blazing logs. But they fell as petals at Siddhartha's feet.

*The **bodhi tree** under which Siddhartha gained enlightenment.*

After the Buddha's enlightenment, the serpent Mucalinda wrapped him in his protective coils.

In the second week after the enlightenment, the Buddha stood without blinking as he meditated on the bodhi tree.

A great temple now stands at Bodh Gaya, the site of the Buddha's enlightenment.

The enlightenment

As a final resort, Mara screamed, "Who will bear witness to your past lives and their generosity?" In reply, Siddhartha put out his right hand and touched the earth and called on the earth to bear witness. With this, Mara was defeated and Siddhartha gained enlightenment. Finally, he saw the truth.

The Teachings

The Buddha did not claim to be a god and did not expect to be worshiped as one. He was a human being who gained enlightenment. He realized that people suffered because they always wanted more. They were never content with what they had. But he also saw that there was a way to end suffering. By realizing the **Four Noble Truths** and following the **Noble Eightfold Path** (another name for the Middle Path), people could overcome greed and desire and achieve enlightenment for themselves.

The wheel of law

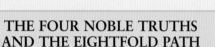

After his enlightenment, the Buddha gave his first talk in a deer park in Sarnath, a town in north India. To explain his teaching, he drew a wheel on the ground. It showed the cycle of birth, death, and rebirth in which everyone is caught. By following the Buddha's teaching, a person could escape from the cycle of rebirth and reach **nirvana**, a state of perfect peace and happiness. By leading a good life, people could move closer to nirvana. A bad life leads them further away.

During a retreat in the Parilyyaka forest, the Buddha was helped by an elephant and a monkey. As a reward, they were reborn in Indra's heaven where Indra showed them the way to salvation.

*The wheel of law is an important Buddhist symbol. It stands for the Buddha himself and the **dharma** he taught.*

In this Tibetan painting, the elephants represent the human spirit as it makes its way toward enlightenment.

THE FOUR NOBLE TRUTHS AND THE EIGHTFOLD PATH

FIRST NOBLE TRUTH: Suffering exists
SECOND NOBLE TRUTH: There is a reason for suffering
THIRD NOBLE TRUTH: There is a way to end suffering
FOURTH NOBLE TRUTH: The way to end suffering is through the Eightfold Path:
1. Right Views
2. Right Thoughts
3. Right Speech
4. Right Action
5. Right Livelihood
6. Right Effort
7. Right Mindfulness
8. Right Concentration

The six states of rebirth shown
inside the wheel are as gods,
as rebel gods, as
ghosts, in hell, as
animals, and as
humans.

Yama, the Lord of the
Dead, holds the wheel
in his teeth and
claws.

The wheel of life
This painting from Tibet shows
Yama, Lord of the Dead, holding up the Wheel
of Life. It represents the cycle of birth, death, and
rebirth which turns like a wheel. Around the outside are
the different stages in a person's life. Inside are six states
into which you might be reborn. In the center are three
animals, representing human faults, which stand in the
way of enlightenment.

The center of the
wheel shows the three
worst faults - greed (the
pig), hatred (the snake), and
delusion (the cock).

The twelve scenes in the outer rim
show the different stages in a human's
life and the consequences of actions.

The black half of the circle shows human
beings destined for hell. The white half
shows those who advance to nirvana.

15

After the Enlightenment

After his enlightenment, the Buddha spent the rest of his life traveling around India, teaching the dharma. He lived as a monk, as did his followers. He also sent his followers out to spread his message. Many people came to hear him and join his band. When the Buddha was about 80 years old, he knew that his life was nearing its end. He called his monks together and made his last journey to Kushinagara. There, in a grove of trees, the Buddha passed away.

*The Buddha teaching his first sermon to two of the five holy men. His hands are in the teaching **mudra** (position).*

The first sermon

The Buddha preached his first sermon after his enlightenment to five holy men in the Deer Park at Sarnath, near the city of Benares. The men had been his companions during his years in the forest. After hearing his teaching, the five holy men gained enlightenment, too.

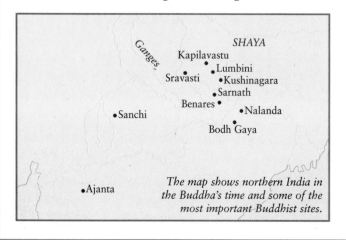

The monastery at Sravasti was paid for by a wealthy merchant, Anathapindada. This medallion shows his servants carrying the gold to pay for the grove.

The first monastery

During the rainy season, the weather made it difficult for the Buddha and his monks to travel. Traditionally, they stayed in a vihara and spent the time meditating and studying. Their most important resting place was located in a grove on the outskirts of the city of Sravasti.

A traveling life

The Buddha and his followers traveled all over northern India, visiting towns and cities on the way. Many of the places they visited have since become important sites for Buddhist pilgrims. One of the holiest sites is Bodh Gaya, where the Buddha gained enlightenment.

Miracle at Sravasti

The Buddha did not normally approve of miracles. But on a visit to Sravasti, he gave a demonstration of his magical powers to win over six rival teachers, making four images of himself appear in a mango tree.

The Buddha also made water jet from his feet and flames from his shoulders, as this statue shows.

The map shows northern India in the Buddha's time and some of the most important Buddhist sites.

The Buddha saying goodbye to Channa, his charioteer, and his favorite horse.

This Tibetan painting shows the Buddha's funeral pyre and the nirvana of the Buddha.

Shortly before his death, the Buddha ate a meal with a woman of lowly birth rather than with a prince, showing that wealth and status did not matter.

The Buddha's funeral

For seven days after the Buddha passed away, there was a wake of music, dances, and offerings of flowers. Then the Buddha's body was taken for cremation. At first, the funeral pyre would not light. But when the disciple, Mahakasyapa, arrived, it burst into flame.

Mahaparinirvana

The image above shows the Buddha's Mahaparinirvana, when he passed away. His work as a Buddha was now done and he could enter the peace of nirvana. Some people describe nirvana as a candle being suddenly blown out.

A bronze statue of a stupa from Tibet.

Cult of relics

After his cremation, the Buddha's ashes were divided into eight and given to eight different groups. **Stupas** were built over them. They became symbols of the Buddha's final nirvana and important places of worship.

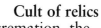
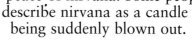

Monks and the Monastic Life

After his enlightenment, the Buddha lived as a monk, traveling around India and inspiring others to join the **sangha,** or community of monks and nuns. Among the first Buddhist monks were the five holy men who had lived in the forest with the Buddha, together with his son, Rahula, and his cousin, Ananda. Today, in Buddhist countries, the sangha is still central to Buddhism. Like the Buddha, some devout Buddhists give up their homes and possessions and dedicate their lives to practicing and teaching the **dharma.** In Mahayana Buddhism, the sangha includes all those who follow the Buddha's teachings, not only monks and nuns.

This terrifying figure is one of the four celestial kings who guard monasteries in Japan.

Head shaving
Buddhist monks wear robes and shave their heads to demonstrate humility and to show that they have given up their attachment to the world. In Sri Lanka and Thailand, monks wear saffron-colored robes. In Tibet, monks' robes are maroon; in Japan, they are black.

Few possessions
Buddhist monks have very few possessions. Traditionally, they are only allowed to own eight items, called Eight Requisites, as listed by the Buddha. These are robes, a belt, an alms' bowl, a razor, a needle and thread, a walking stick, a water strainer, and a toothpick.

Receiving alms
In **Theravada** countries, such as Sri Lanka, monks rely on local people for their food, just as in the Buddha's day. Every morning, devotees fill the monks' bowls with food. The monks take it back to the monastery and share it out among themselves.

Below: In this painting from Myanmar, the Buddha receives alms in his bowl from a rich merchant.

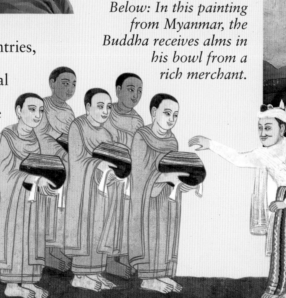

Above and right (next page): monks in a Tibetan monastery go about their daily lives. For Buddhists, the flame of a candle indicates the light of enlightenment.

Translating texts

As Buddhism spread from India, the sacred texts had to be translated into other languages, such as Tibetan or Chinese. It was a long and difficult task and the monks who performed it were greatly respected. In the painting on the right, they are being watched over by various **bodhisattvas**.

Ordination

In some Buddhist countries, young boys spend several months in a monastery as part of their education. Some will become monks. They must obey a set of monastic rules, called the **vinaya**.

Above: A young Theravada monk being ordained in Cambodia. The older man wears a white sash to show that he is a lay Buddhist, and not a monk.

A monastery

The Potala (right) was built on a sacred hill near Lhasa, in Tibet. It was the traditional home of the Dalai Lama, the spiritual leader of Tibet's Buddhists.

The Potala has over a thousand rooms, including a great assembly hall for monks and pilgrims, a monastery, and living quarters.

Life in the monastery

Monks and nuns live strict, simple lives. They spend their time studying, chanting, and discussing the Buddhist scriptures, learning to meditate, and teaching the Buddha's message. They also run and care for the monastery, and organize religious ceremonies and festivals. Some monks help in the local community.

Buddhism Splits and Spreads

After the Buddha passed away, his teachings were memorized by his followers and passed down by word of mouth. A council was called to collect his teachings together. About a hundred years later, a second council took place to set out the rules of discipline for Buddhist monks and nuns. But different opinions began to arise about what the Buddha actually taught, and Buddhism split into two main schools of thought. They were called **Theravada**, meaning "Way of the Elders," and **Mahayana**, meaning "Great Vehicle." Gradually, these two schools spread outside of India.

Bodhisattvas are perfect beings who gain enlightenment but put off reaching nirvana to help other people.

Mahayana

Mahayana Buddhism spread northwest from India to Nepal, Tibet, China, Japan, Korea, and Vietnam. Its followers believe in many different Buddhas and godlike figures, called bodhisattvas. They include lay Buddhists as well as monks as part of the sangha (community), and value both highly.

This beautiful image, with its flowing robes, shows how Buddhist art was greatly influenced by the Greeks. This style is called Gandharan, after a region in northwest India.

King Milinda, the Greek

A Greek king, Milinda (Menandros) ruled India in the 2nd century BCE. He is famous for a conversation he had with a Buddhist monk. As a result, Milinda converted to Buddhism. Their conversation became part of the Buddhist scriptures.

Map showing the spread of Buddhism across Asia, with locations including:

MONGOLIA, Kyoto, Pyogyang, Nara, Datong, Kucha, Kashgar, Wanfosi, Peshawar, Miran, Niya, Hangzhou, Hadda, Changsha, Chengdu, Meerut, Lhasa, Sarnath, Bodh Gaya, Dali, Guangzhou, Pagan, Hanoi, Ajanta, Pegu, Elephanta, Sukhothai, Amaravati, Ayutthaya, Angkor, Kanchipuram, Anwadhapura, Kandi, BORNEO, Palembang, Borobudur, Indus

Key to map

- Area of origin of Buddhism
- → Early spread of Buddhism
- → Mahayana Buddhism
- → Theravada Buddhism
- → Tantric Buddhism
- ✦ Rock-carved temple
- ▲ Sacred mountain

Buddha

Theravada

Mahayana
Japanese sects
Ch'an -Zen
Vajrayana - Lamaism

Shinto and Japanese traditions
Chinese meditative practice
Tantrism, occult, Tibetan Bon

The diagram above shows how Buddhism split into its two main groups.

Theravada

Theravada Buddhism spread southward to Sri Lanka, Myanmar, Thailand, Cambodia, and Laos. Its followers use the teachings of Siddhartha Gautama, the historical Buddha whom they believe was a human being, although a very special one. They also believe that the sangha of monks and monastic life are very important.

Buddhism in India

The great Indian emperor, Ashoka, ruled from 269–231 BCE. He became a Buddhist after a particularly bloody battle in which 100,000 people were killed. Filled with remorse, Ashoka vowed to follow the Buddhist way of peace and nonviolence. He sent his missionaries far and wide to spread the Buddha's teachings.

Tibetan woman with Buddhist prayer wheel.

Head of the Buddha in Gandharan style.

Buddhism in Tibet

Buddhism was introduced into Tibet from India in the 7th century CE. Two of King Songtsen Gampo's wives were devout Buddhists who persuaded him to convert. With the help of the great Indian teacher, Padmasambhava, Buddhism became the official religion of Tibet in the 8th century.

Buddhism in the Far East

Buddhism spread north-eastward from India along the Silk Road. It first reached China in the 1st century AD, although it did not become established for another 400 years. Buddhism reached Japan from Korea in the 6th century CE.

This bronze Buddhist figure was cast in Korea in the 7th century CE.

Buddhism in Sri Lanka

Buddhism reached Sri Lanka in about 250 BCE when Emperor Ashoka sent his son, Mahinda, a Buddhist monk, to the island. The Sri Lankan king converted to Buddhism and most of the island soon followed him.

This Buddha's head comes from Cambodia. Almost 90 percent of Cambodians are Buddhists.

Monks in Thailand

Since the 13th century CE, Buddhism has been the official religion of Thailand. More than 90 percent of its population are Buddhists. There are close links between the government and the sangha of monks. Traditionally, every young Thai boy spends some time as a monk as part of his education.

Artistic styles

As Buddhism spread out of India, it inspired many different styles of art. Each country's artists produced beautiful sculptures and paintings of the Buddha and of scenes from his life. This 6th-century Chinese statue shows how the rounded, fleshy forms of the Indian tradition became flatter and more angular in China.

Buddhist Texts

For hundreds of years after his death, the Buddha's teachings were passed on by word of mouth. They were not written down until the first century BCE. The oldest writings are the Pali Canon, the sacred texts of Theravada Buddhists. The Pali Canon is also called the *Tipitaka*, or Three Baskets. The first basket contains rules for monks and nuns. The second contains the Buddha's teachings. The third contains discussions of the teachings. Mahayana Buddhists have their own set of scriptures. Many of these are called **sutras**, or "threads." They include teachings and stories of the Buddha and other monks.

Above: A monk studying the scriptures.

Below: A volume of the Kanjur.

Right: An 18th century Chinese illustration of a scene from the Tipitaka.

A page from a 9th–10th century illustrated version of the Lotus Sutra, written in Chinese.

The Kanjur

The Kanjur is a large collection of scriptures sacred to Tibetan Buddhists. The word Kanjur means "the translated word of the Buddha." The collection contains teachings believed to have come directly from the historical Buddha. The original scriptures came from India and were translated into Tibetan by Buddhist monks.

Monks copied and translated the sacred texts. Their job was very difficult because they had to translate totally new words and ideas into their own languages.

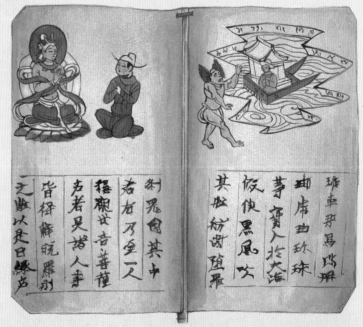

The Lotus Sutra

The Lotus Sutra is one of the most important Mahayana texts. A long volume of poetry, sermons, and stories, it explains that everyone has the potential to reach enlightenment and become a buddha.

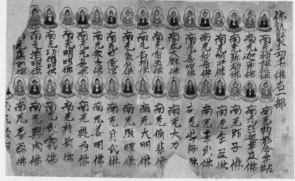

Part of an ancient Chinese text, illustrated with rows of Buddhas.

Books and libraries

Buddhist texts were traditionally written on handmade paper, cut into rectangular pages. The pages were bound in silk between two wooden boards (see above). The books were stored in great libraries in the monasteries (below).

Pilgrims and texts

As Buddhism spread, Chinese monks made long and risky journeys to India to collect sacred texts. They took these back to China where they translated them into Chinese. The famous 7th-century monk, Xuan-zang, is said to have needed 20 horses to carry back all the Buddhist texts he had collected.

This Chinese painting shows Xuan-zang on his return from India in 645 CE with priceless Buddhist icons and manuscripts.

Lotus stones

Tibetan Buddhists carve **mantras** (sacred words) on piles of stones to express their wishes to the gods. Some stones are inscribed with the famous mantra *"Om mani padme hum."* This means "the jewel in the lotus."

Wall paintings, like this painting of a demon from Myanmar, were used to help spread the Buddha's teachings to people who could not read.

Buddhism in Sri Lanka

Buddhism reached Sri Lanka in about 250 BCE, making it the first country outside India to which Buddhism spread. Tradition says that the Sri Lankan king, Tissa, sent a messenger to Emperor Ashoka requesting friendship between their two countries. In reply, Ashoka sent his son, Milinda, a Buddhist monk, and four others to Sri Lanka to teach Buddhism to the king. King Tissa converted to Buddhism and soon afterward most of the islanders followed him. A sangha and monastery were founded, and holy relics were brought from India, including a cutting from the sacred bodhi tree beneath which the Buddha meditated.

The map shows the island of Sri Lanka and its key Buddhist sites and sacred places.

Island people

About 80 percent of Sri Lankan people are Sinhalese, such as the man on the right. Most of them are Buddhists. They are thought to have reached Sri Lanka from northeast India in the 5th century BCE. Other important groups include Hindu Tamils, with some Christians and Muslims.

The four-lion head of the Ashokan column at Sarnath in India is the emblem of modern India.

Ashoka's missionaries

During the reign of Emperor Ashoka (c. 273–232 BCE), Buddhism enjoyed a golden age in India. Ashoka's missionaries, including his own son and daughter, helped spread the Buddha's teaching to Sri Lanka and other countries outside India.

King Parakramabahu I

The statue below shows King Parakramabahu I who ruled Sri Lanka in the mid-12th century CE. After defeating the Hindu Tamils from India, he helped Buddhism to revive on the island and built many new monasteries and stupas in the new capital of Polonnaruwa (see next page).

Meditation

Meditation is a very important part of Buddhist practice. Buddhists believe that training their minds will bring them closer to enlightenment. Buddhists use these colored disks on the wall of a Sri Lankan monastery to help them concentrate and clear their minds for meditation.

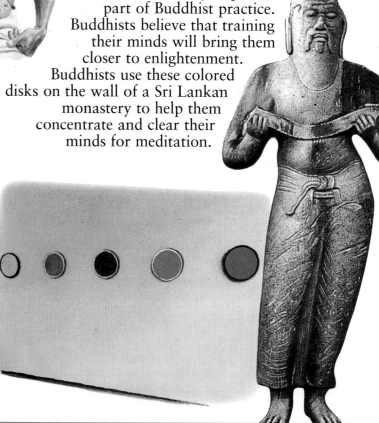

A monk
praying in front of a
painted stone Buddha
at Anuradhapura.
The image shows the Buddha's parinirvana.

Polonnaruwa

In the 11th century CE, the capital of Sri Lanka moved from Anarudhapura to Polonnaruwa. Here King Parakramabahu built an enormous complex with many monasteries and monuments. Among these are two huge statues of the Buddha meditating and of his **parinirvana,** carved out of the rock.

The traditional emblem of Sri Lanka which appears on a moonstone in a monastery in the Polonnaruwa complex.

Buddhism today

Today, Buddhism, in its Theravada form, is still the religion of most of the Sinhalese people of Sri Lanka. They are proud of its ancient tradition. New temples, such as the one shown below, are still being built to honor the Buddha.

Monks in Sri Lanka

In Sri Lanka today, the sangha still plays an important part in the island's life and monks are treated with great respect. There are about 15,000 monks in Sri Lanka. Some are active in education and social work. Some have even acted as advisers to the country's leaders and politicians.

Anuradhapura

In King Tissa's time, the capital of Sri Lanka was Anuradhapura. Today, pilgrims still travel to the ancient city to visit the sacred bodhi tree, said to have grown from a cutting of the original bodhi tree in Bodh Gaya and brought to Sri Lanka by Ashoka's daughter, a Buddhist nun.

A casket from Sri Lanka, decorated with rubies and gold. It shows the Buddha sitting on a throne, teaching.

Two figures attending the Buddha from the monastery of Gangarama Vihara in Colombo, Sri Lanka.

Buddha Images and Stupas

The earliest works of Buddhist art were cave paintings and carvings, showing scenes from the Buddha's life. The Buddha was never shown in person but by symbols, such as a wheel, a footprint, or a **bodhi tree**. As Buddhism spread out of India, many different art styles developed. Images of the Buddha were made for temples and monasteries. But the images are not just for decoration. They show a variety of signs which mark the Buddha as a very special person. Stupas are Buddhist monuments which represent the Buddhist universe. The first **stupas** were built to house the Buddha's ashes after his death.

A carving of a hand held in the peaceful and protective gesture of the Abhaya mudra.

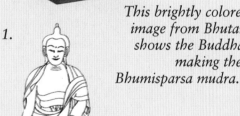

This brightly colored image from Bhutan shows the Buddha making the Bhumisparsa mudra.

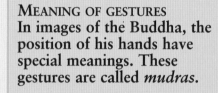

MEANING OF GESTURES
In images of the Buddha, the position of his hands have special meanings. These gestures are called *mudras*.

1. BHUMISPARSA MUDRA: calling the earth to witness;
2. ABHAYA MUDRA: to calm fear and give protection;
3. DHARMACHAKRA MUDRA: teaching the dharma;
4. VITARKA MUDRA: discussing the dharma;
5. VARADA MUDRA: compassion and granting of a wish;
6. DHYANA MUDRA: balance and meditation; concentrating on the dharma;
7. CHIKEN-IN: the fist of wisdom; the importance of knowledge in the spiritual world.

1.
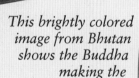

2.

3.

4.

5.

6.

7.

Stupa styles

The first stupas, built in India, were shaped like domes. Gradually, as Buddhism spread to other countries, different shapes and styles developed. In China and Japan, stupas turned into tall, pointed pagodas. In Sri Lanka, stupas are called dagobas. In Tibet, they are called chortens.

The reclining Buddha

Many images show the Buddha lying on his side because this is how he passed away (Buddhists do not say that he died). Buddhists describe his passing away as **parinirvana**.

The Buddha is always shown with a jeweled topknot on his head.

Below: This Japanese statue shows the birth of the Buddha as he emerges from the sleeve of his mother's gown.

This huge Buddha image at Kamakura, Japan, holds his hands in the Dhyana mudra (6).

This Nepalese stupa has a more rounded shape than those found in Southeast Asia.

There are four different types of stupa: those with ashes or relics belonging to the Buddha; those with relics of important monks; those built to commemorate an event; and those built by lay people to gain merit.

27

Chinese Buddhism

Buddhism spread into China along the Silk Road in the 1st century CE when Buddhist monks from India and central Asia began to establish themselves. By the 6th century, Mahayana Buddhism had become one of China's three main religions (see below). Many people were attracted to its teachings about suffering, rebirth, and nirvana. Donations from wealthy followers, and even from the royal family itself, paid for the building of great temples and monasteries. In this way, devotees hoped to earn merit to help them on the journey toward enlightenment. These monasteries and temples became important centers of Buddhist teaching, scholarship, and charity.

Chinese pilgrims
Chinese monks traveled to India to learn more about Buddhism and visit the places where the Buddha had lived. Hsuan Tang (above) reached India in about CE 630. He spent time at the great Buddhist monastery of Nalanda, studying the sacred texts. He returned to China fifteen years later, laden down with religious objects and texts.

In this painting, Lao-tzu and Confucius protect the baby Siddhartha, the future Buddha.

Three faiths
When Buddhism reached China, the religions of **Confucianism**, founded by the great teacher Confucius, and **Taoism**, founded by Lao-tzu, were already well established. Over the centuries, many similarities developed between the three traditions as their beliefs, ideas, and teachings merged and mixed together.

Different schools
Many different schools of Mahayana Buddhism developed in China. One of the most important schools is called Pure Land. The Pure Land is a beautiful, peaceful place, ruled by the bodhisattva Amitabha. Buddhists who worship Amitabha hope to be reborn in the Pure Land on their way to nirvana. They chant his name to help them.

An Amitabha Buddha from the Sui Dynasty (6th century).

Box pagodas
The ancient stone pagoda shown on the left is carved with Buddhist scriptures and images of the Buddha. Thousands of pagodas like this were built to hold copies of the sutras.

Buddhist art

In China, Buddhism inspired many beautiful works of art. The monks and traders who brought Buddhism to China also brought Greek and Indian influences with them. These mixed with Chinese artistic styles. Chinese artists produced stone sculptures, exquisite gold and silverware, painting, and embroideries to decorate temples and monasteries.

Many Buddhas

In China, the bodhisattvas of Mahayana Buddhism took on different forms and names. For example, the **bodhisattva** of compassion, Avalokiteshvara, became known as Guanyin (left). Another important bodhisattva was Amitabha, the ruler of the Pure Land (see previous page).

A silver container from the 9th century CE for holding a relic of the Buddha. It shows a bodhisattva kneeling on a lotus throne.

Cave temples

In the 5th and 6th centuries AD, huge Buddhist temples were carved in cliffside caves. The walls of the caves were decorated with massive images and paintings of the Buddha, the bodhisattvas, and scenes from the Buddha's life. The images above can be seen in a cave at Longmen.

Left: A statue of a Lohan, or "worthy one." He sits cross-legged in meditation.

Worthy ones

In Chinese Buddhism, a person who had gained enlightenment is called a **Lohan**, or "worthy one." Chinese texts tell of eighteen disciples of the Buddha who became Lohan, including the Buddha's own son. The Lohan were honored for their skill in meditation and in teaching the dharma, and for their magical powers.

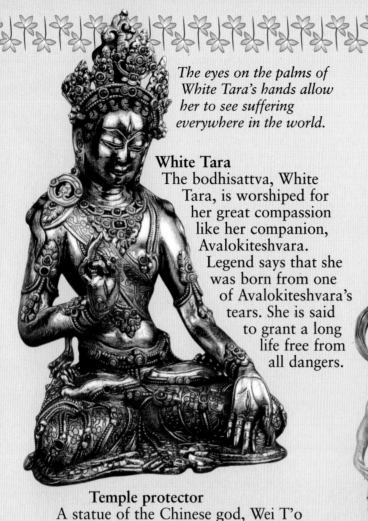

The eyes on the palms of White Tara's hands allow her to see suffering everywhere in the world.

White Tara

The bodhisattva, White Tara, is worshiped for her great compassion like her companion, Avalokiteshvara. Legend says that she was born from one of Avalokiteshvara's tears. She is said to grant a long life free from all dangers.

Temple protector

A statue of the Chinese god, Wei T'o (below) guards the sanctuary of every Chinese Buddhist temple. Wei T'o stands with his back to the main entrance, facing the altar. He destroys any demons who try to creep into the temple.

This painting shows Wei T'o as a soldier in armor with a spiked helmet and a club for destroying the demons.

Celestial beings

Gandharvas are heavenly musicians. They also help to carry over a person's actions and their consquences between their death and their next rebirth. They are sometimes shown in paintings flying over the Buddha.

Vajradhara

Vajradhara is often shown with a thunderbolt (vajra) in one hand and a bell in the other. The vajra symbolizes the power of compassion. The bell symbolizes the pure sound of wisdom

Kannon

Kannon is the Japanese form of one of the most popular bodhisattvas. Also called Avalokiteshvara and Guanyin, he is worshiped for his compassion. Here he is shown with a crown of eleven heads which represent his virtues.

Kannon with eleven heads.

Gods and Goddesses

Buddhists do not believe in an all-powerful god who created the world and cares for it and to whom you pray for help. The Buddha did not claim to be a god and did not want to be worshiped as one. He was a human being, though an extraordinary one, who helped other people live better lives through his teaching and example. But Mahayana Buddhists also worship godlike figures, called bodhisattvas. These are perfect, heavenly beings who have gained **enlightenment** but put off entering **nirvana** in order to help other people.

A gandharva carrying a lotus blossom.

Avalokiteshvara
One of the most popular bodhisattvas, Avalokiteshvara, represents perfect compassion. He not only tries to lead people toward enlightenment but to help them with problems in their everyday lives. Because of his magical powers, he can appear in many forms, as a buddha, a woman, a beggar, or as a god.

Right: Painting of a protector of the faith and a god who distributes wealth from the northern Sakya monastery in Tibet. It dates to the 13th century, when this monastery was at its most powerful.

Above: A Japanese statue of Avalokiteshvara. He is dressed as a monk, with a pilgrim's staff and a magic jewel.

Right: A statue of Jizo, the Japanese form of Ksitigarbha.

King of hell
The bodhisattva Ksitigarbha is the master of the six worlds of desire and the six states of rebirth. He is also the bodhisattva of hell. Moved by compassion, he consoles those beings who go to hell because of evil action in their past lives, and tries to lighten their burden.

Brahma, the creator
This Burmese carving shows the Hindu god Brahma, the creator. After the Buddha's enlightenment, legend says, Brahma encouraged him to go out and teach people what he had learned, saying, "Now that you, O sage, have crossed the ocean of the world of becoming, rescue other living beings who have sunk so low in suffering."

Mother goddess
In China, Avalokiteshvara becomes the goddess Guanyin, "she who hears the sound of the world." Worshiped for her compassion and mercy, she is often shown wearing long robes and carrying a child in one arm. Festivals are held every year to celebrate her birth, enlightenment, and death.

Right: The Bodhisattva Guanyin.

Buddhism in Southeast Asia

Buddhism has a long history in Southeast Asia. It has flourished in Myanmar (Burma) since at least the 2nd century BCE when Buddhist monks from Myanmar were reported attending a ceremony in Sri Lanka. Until the 11th century, Buddhism competed with **Hinduism,** but then became the country's main religion. Buddhism may have been taken to Thailand by Indian traders in the early centuries CE. It slowly became established and, by the end of the 13th century, it had become the official religion not only in Thailand but also in neighboring Cambodia and Laos. Today, Buddhism, in its Theravada form, is still the official religion of these three countries.

The map shows the countries of Southeast Asia. Theravada Buddhism is strongest today in Myanmar, Thailand, Cambodia, and Laos. Islam has taken over from Buddhism in Malaysia and Indonesia.

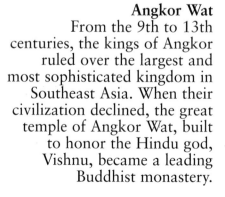

Reconstruction of the ancient temple of Angkor Wat, located in modern Cambodia.

Fearsome creatures like this stand guard outside Buddhist temples in Thailand. They date from pre-Buddhist times.

Angkor Wat
From the 9th to 13th centuries, the kings of Angkor ruled over the largest and most sophisticated kingdom in Southeast Asia. When their civilization declined, the great temple of Angkor Wat, built to honor the Hindu god, Vishnu, became a leading Buddhist monastery.

Temple roofs in Thailand are decorated with graceful chofas which imitate the shape of a swan's neck.

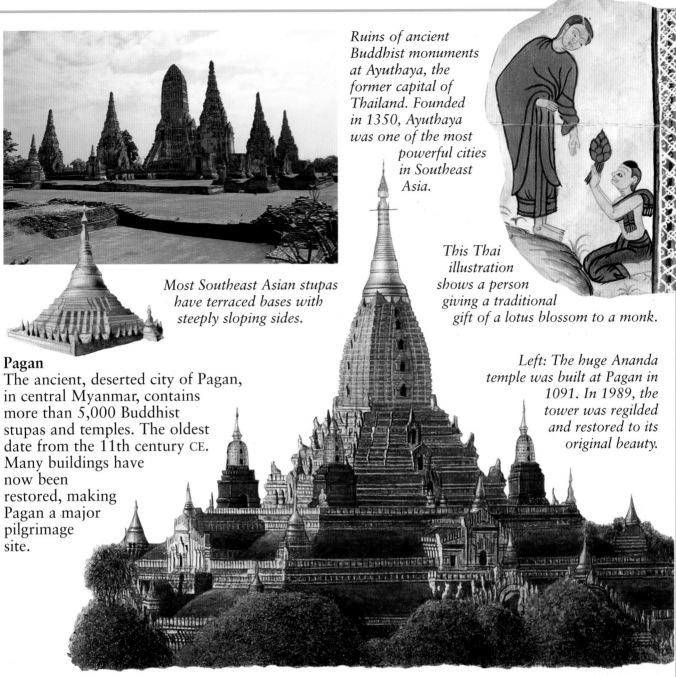

Ruins of ancient Buddhist monuments at Ayuthaya, the former capital of Thailand. Founded in 1350, Ayuthaya was one of the most powerful cities in Southeast Asia.

Most Southeast Asian stupas have terraced bases with steeply sloping sides.

This Thai illustration shows a person giving a traditional gift of a lotus blossom to a monk.

Pagan

The ancient, deserted city of Pagan, in central Myanmar, contains more than 5,000 Buddhist stupas and temples. The oldest date from the 11th century CE. Many buildings have now been restored, making Pagan a major pilgrimage site.

Left: The huge Ananda temple was built at Pagan in 1091. In 1989, the tower was regilded and restored to its original beauty.

Borobodur

The massive Buddhist monument of Borobodur in Java was built in the early 9th century CE. When Buddhism declined, Borobodur was abandoned and only rediscovered in 1814. Shaped like a stepped pyramid with a stupa on top, each of its terraces represents a stage towards enlightenment in a person's life.

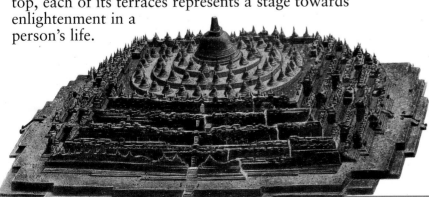

The terraces at Borobodur are decorated with images of the Buddha and carvings, like the ones above, of Buddhist teachings and stories.

33

Zen Buddhism

One of the best-known schools of Japanese Buddhism, Zen was founded by an Indian monk, Bodhidharma, and brought from China to Japan. The word Zen means "meditation." Zen Buddhists have many ways of meditating to help them focus and clear their minds.

Left: This print shows a Zen tea ceremony. The ceremony follows complicated rules and etiquette which bring a sense of harmony and tranquility.

Japan and Korea

Buddhism arrived in Japan from Korea in the 6th century CE. One of the kings of Korea sent a mission to the Japanese emperor, asking for help in a war. Among the gifts he sent was an image of the Buddha. Under Prince Shotoku (ruled 592–621), Buddhism flourished. From the 7th century, Chinese Buddhism reached Japan and many different Buddhist groups developed. Some of the biggest and most important are **Tendai, Pure Land,** and **Zen.** Today, about three quarters of Japanese people are Buddhists. Some people follow a mixture of Buddhism and Shinto, the ancient religion of Japan, and in many places, Buddhist temples stand alongside Shinto shrines.

A statue of Prince Shotoku worshiping the Buddha. He helped to establish Buddhism in Japan.

Gods of fortune
The god Daikoku (left) is one of the seven gods of good fortune. Originally these were Buddhist gods but they are now worshiped in the Shinto religion, too.

Ritsu
The Ritsu school of Buddhism, founded in China, was mainly concerned with the rules of monastic and religious practice.

Daikoku is the god of wealth and farming. He is shown sitting on a large sack of rice. His attendant is a rat who nibbles at the rice.

An image of the Buddha carved from rock in South Korea.

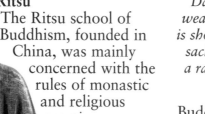

Shinkai (1229–1304) was a specialist Ritsu monk.

In Korea
Buddhism reached Korea from China in the 6th century CE, and was adopted as its official religion. After World War II, Korea split into north and south. Buddhism was almost wiped out in North Korea but is still strong in the south.

34

Nichiren Buddhism

The monk Nichiren (1222–82) founded a Japanese school of Buddhism which is based on the *Lotus Sutra* (see page 22). He fiercely criticized other Buddhist groups and was banished to the island of Izu. The print (right) shows Nichiren calming the sea on his way to exile.

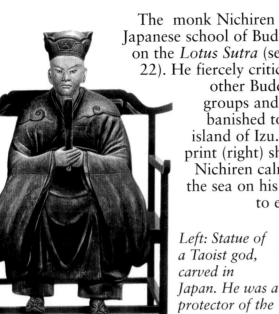

Left: Statue of a Taoist god, carved in Japan. He was a protector of the monastery.

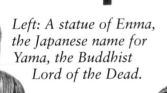

Mikkyo

Mikkyo, a branch of "esoteric Buddhism," was introduced to Japan during the 9th century CE. It gradually replaced the Tendai school. Esoteric Buddhism was even stronger in the earlier Shingon school of Buddhism, founded by Kukai (774–835 CE).

Left: A statue of Enma, the Japanese name for Yama, the Buddhist Lord of the Dead.

Pure Land

The Pure Land school of Buddhism is popular in Japan, Korea, and China (see page 28). Its followers worship the bodhisattva, Amitabha. He is known as Amida in Japan and as Amit' a-bul in Korea (see below).

A bell and three vajras (thunderbolts). Liturgical instruments like this were used during religious rituals in Mikkyo Buddhism.

Right: Amit'a-bul, the Buddha of the Infinite Light, governs the Pure Land or, Western Paradise.

Zen art and calligraphy

Traditionally, Zen Buddhists do not believe in using images of the Buddha in their practice. But art and calligraphy (beautiful writing) play an important part. They are believed to help followers train their minds into a Buddha-like state.

This fragment from a Buddhist scroll was painted in the 13th or 14th century. It shows a monk burning an image of the Buddha, saying that it is simply a piece of wood.

Practicing Buddhism

Buddhists try to follow the Buddha's teachings in everything they do. They make a commitment to the Three Jewels (see page 38) by saying the words: "I go to the Buddha for refuge; I go to the dharma for refuge; I go to the sangha for refuge." They also make five promises, called the **Five Precepts**. They promise not to harm or kill living things, not to steal or take anything that is not freely given, to control sexual desire, not to tell lies or speak unkindly, and not to drink alcohol or take drugs.

Prayer wheels

The Tibetan Buddhist above spins a prayer wheel in his right hand. The prayer wheel is a metal cylinder with a tiny paper scroll inside on which thousands of prayers are written. By spinning the wheel, the man releases the prayers into the world. Huge prayer wheels are found in Tibetan temples.

Buddha image

Every Buddhist shrine, at home or in the temple, has an image of the Buddha. The image reminds people of the Buddha's teaching and of his special qualities of calmness, wisdom, and compassion. In early Buddhist art, the Buddha was not shown in person but by symbols, such as a footprint like this one.

Meditation

The Buddha gained enlightenment while meditating under the bodhi tree. Buddhists try to follow his example. By meditating, they hope to calm their minds and gain knowledge. Most Buddhists try to meditate every day.

The bodhi tree

The bodhi tree was the tree under which the Buddha gained enlightenment. The tree in Bodh Gaya, India, is said to be descended from the original tree. It is the custom to plant a bodhi tree in a Buddhist monastery to represent the dharma.

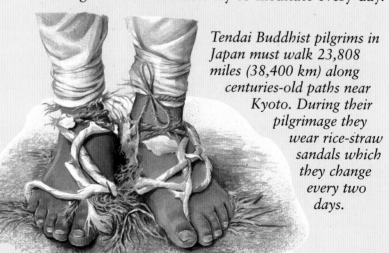

Tendai Buddhist pilgrims in Japan must walk 23,808 miles (38,400 km) along centuries-old paths near Kyoto. During their pilgrimage they wear rice-straw sandals which they change every two days.

Mount Kailash in the Himalayas is an important pilgrimage site for Tibetan Buddhists.

Pilgrimage

The places linked with the Buddha's life are important pilgrimage sites. The holiest are the Buddha's birthplace in Lumbini, Bodh Gaya where he gained enlightenment, Sarnath where he gave his first sermon, and Kushinagara where he passed away. By making a pilgrimage, Buddhists hope to earn merit to help them in their next lives.

Good qualities

The Buddha taught that wisdom, morality, and meditation were very important qualities. People should also be generous, kind, and compassionate in their dealings with others. These qualities will help people to lead a good life and move closer to enlightenment.

This Tibetan prayer bell symbolizes wisdom. It is rung during some Buddhist ceremonies.

Buddhist puja

These Buddhists are paying their respects to the Buddha in the Jokhang Temple in Lhasa, Tibet. This practice is called puja. As part of the **puja**, they chant sacred verses and place offerings on the shrine (see below).

Extreme practice

Some Buddhist monks follow Siddhartha's example and leave the world behind. They retreat to a forest or cave to live a simple, solitary life of meditation.

Inside this cave is a monk. As he counts off his prayer beads, he chants the name of the Buddha. This helps him to meditate.

Making offerings

Each of the offerings has a special meaning. Flowers look bright and fresh but eventually die. This is a reminder of the Buddha's teaching that nothing lasts forever. Candles represent the light of enlightenment. The sweet smell of incense is like the dharma.

Tibetan Buddhism

Buddhism came to Tibet from India in the 7th century CE, during the reign of King Songsten Gamp (605–650). Encouraged by his two Buddhist wives, he became a Buddhist. A long struggle followed between Buddhism and Bon, the ancient religion of Tibet. Its followers worshiped many gods and spirits, using magic to keep them happy. Many Buddhists were persecuted. By the 14th century, however, Buddhism had become the main religion of Tibet. Tibetans follow a type of Buddhism which mixes Mahayana and Tantric beliefs (see below). Apart from the historical Buddha, they worship many bodhisattvas, the most important of which is Avalokiteshvara.

A bronze image of Padmasambhava from the 17th–18th century.

Padmasambhava

Padmasambhava was a great teacher of Buddhism who came to Tibet from India in the 8th century. He helped to spread Buddhism to the ordinary people. During his time, the first Buddhist monastery was built in Tibet and the first Buddhist monks ordained. His name means "lotus born."

Tantric Buddhism

Tantric Buddhism is a type of Indian Buddhism which uses magic and rituals to help people achieve enlightenment. It gets its name from the **Tantras**, a collection of mysterious sacred texts. Followers meditate and chant mantras, powerful sacred sounds and words.

Below: An 18th century Indian painting showing the fearsome Hindu goddess, Kali. Many Hindu gods and goddesses appear in Tantric Buddhism.

Worship in Tibet

Tibetan Buddhists visit monasteries and temples to make offerings, chant mantras, and perform puja. They walk around the temple three times, in a clockwise direction, to remember the Three Jewels. As they walk, they spin **prayer wheels** to release the prayers inside.

Tibet before China's invasion
Tibet today

Tibet today

In the 1950s, the Chinese army invaded Tibet and Tibet became part of China. Hundreds of monasteries were destroyed, precious books burned, and priceless treasures smashed. Thousands of monks were imprisoned and killed. Many Tibetan Buddhists now live as refugees in India.

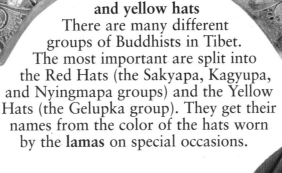

This headdress shows the five Buddhas of Meditation. They represent goodness, knowledge, speech, action, and wisdom.

A Tibetan lama's ritual headdress which is worn at festivals and ceremonies.

Mandalas

The circular picture below is called a **mandala**. The mandala represents the sacred world. Each part has a special meaning, with colors, shapes, and figures standing for different qualities. Concentrating on the details helps Tibetan Buddhists to meditate.

Red hats and yellow hats

There are many different groups of Buddhists in Tibet. The most important are split into the Red Hats (the Sakyapa, Kagyupa, and Nyingmapa groups) and the Yellow Hats (the Gelupka group). They get their names from the color of the hats worn by the **lamas** on special occasions.

Right: The present Dalai Lama, Tenzin Gyatso, was born in 1935. Since 1959, he has lived in exile in India.

The Dalai Lama

Until the Chinese invasion, the Dalai Lama was Tibet's religious leader and also head of the government. He is believed to be the reincarnation of the bodhisattva Avalokiteshvara. When a Dalai Lama dies, Avalokiteshvara's spirt is reborn into the body of a baby who becomes the next Dalai Lama.

The Potala Palace

The huge Potala Palace (see right) stands on a sacred hill, overlooking Lhasa, the capital of Tibet. This was the Dalai Lama's home. The name Potala comes from the legendary mountain home of the bodhisattva **Avalokiteshvara**.

Buddhist Festivals and Celebrations

Throughout the year, there are many Buddhists festivals and celebrations. The most important mark special times in the Buddha's life, such as his birthday and enlightenment. Others remember bodhisattvas, teachers, or events from Buddhist history. Some festivals are celebrated by Buddhists all over the world. But they vary from country to country, depending on a country's own customs and culture, and from Buddhist group to Buddhist group. Other festivals are unique to one particular country. Festivals are happy, optimistic times for Buddhists. Many Buddhists visit their local monastery to pay their respects to the Buddha and take gifts and donations for the monks.

Full Moon days
Most important Buddhist festivals are held at the time of the full moon. These are particularly holy for Buddhists because the main events in the Buddha's life, such as his birth and enlightenment, are said to have happened on full moon times.

Sacred tooth
In August, a special parade of elephants takes place in Kandy, Sri Lanka. The largest elephant carries a golden stupa which contains a very precious relic – a sacred tooth, said to have belonged to the Buddha.

Tibetan monks blowing their ceremonial horns as part of a religious festival.

Right: This festival in Japan remembers how a proud Buddhist monk was once turned into a frog.

Tibetan festivals
Traditionally, Tibetan festivals were colorful occasions when huge crowds gathered in the monastery courtyard. Today, celebrations are much smaller but festivals are still marked by Tibetan refugees in India and elsewhere.

Happy New Year
Losar is a Tibetan festival which marks the start of the New Year in February. This is a time for new beginnings when people spring-clean their houses and scare away evil spirits left over from the previous year. People visit the monasteries and remember the Buddha's early life.

Rains retreat

During the rainy season in countries such as Thailand and Sri Lanka, the monks spend time in their monasteries, studying and meditating. A special festival called Kathina marks the end of the rains in October or November.

O-bon

O-bon is a Japanese Mahayana festival celebrated in July. It is a family festival to honor the ancestors. People place herbs and flowers on the family shrine, and light small fires to welcome the ancestors' spirits home (see above). There is dancing and a special feast. Then the spirits depart again.

The Buddha's birthday

The most important festival in the Theravada calendar is Wesak, which falls on the full moon of May. This is the happiest day of the year, when people celebrate the Buddha's birth, enlightenment and passing away. People visit the monastery and decorate their homes with lamps and flowers. Some people exchange Wesak cards.

In Japan, the Buddha's birthday is celebrated on April 8. Bathing an image of the Buddha with scented water is traditional on his birthday.

Left: In Thailand, a festival of lights marks the end of the rains' retreat. Images like this one are paraded through the streets on their way to the monastery.

Above: A Buddhist festival in Buryat, Russia, in July. All religions, including Buddhism, were discouraged in Russia under Communist rule. But since the collapse of the Soviet Union in the early 1990s, religious practices and celebrations have flourished.

41

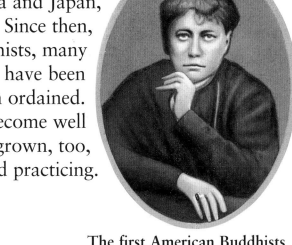

The knot of eternity, a Buddhist symbol from a monastery in Vermont.

Buddhism in the West

At the end of the 19th century, Buddhism reached the West through the writings of Western scholars and their translations of Buddhist texts. It was also spread by people from Buddhist countries, such as China and Japan, who came to live in the West. Since then, thousands of people have become Buddhists, many Buddhist monasteries, temples, and centers have been built, and many monks and nuns have been ordained. Traditional groups, such as Zen, have become well established. But new Buddhist groups have grown, too, with new ways of thinking and practicing.

The first American Buddhists
Colonel Henry Steel Olcott (1832–1907) and Helena Blavatsky (1831–91, above) may have been the first Americans formally to become Buddhists. On a visit to Sri Lanka in 1880, they went to a temple and committed themselves to the Three Jewels and repeated the Five Precepts before a Buddhist monk.

Left: Members of the Pali Text Society, including T.W. and Caroline Rhys Davids.

Translating Buddhist texts
In 1881, the Pali Text Society was founded by scholars, T. W. and Caroline Rhys Davids. The Rhys Davids became interested in Buddhism while working for the British Civil Service in Sri Lanka (then Ceylon). The Society collected, translated, and published Theravada Buddhist scriptures in Great Britain, introducing many people to Buddhism.

Buddhism in Great Britain
British Buddhism began in the late 19th century with a man called Alan Bennett. He traveled to Myanmar and became a Buddhist monk, Ananda Maitreya. He helped to found the first Buddhist Society in Britain. In 1926, a Sri Lankan, Anagarika Dharmapala, founded the London Buddhist Vihara, the first Buddhist center outside Asia.

Right: The cover of the first issue of the Buddhist Review, published in London in 1926.

BUDDHISM IN ENGLAND

VOL. 1.   NO. 1.

AUM MANI PASME HUM

Buddhist groups in the USA

In the last 80 years, many Americans have become Buddhists. Many have joined Zen Buddhist groups, set up by Zen masters from Japan and Korea. Zen is one of the longest established Buddhist traditions in the USA. Tibetan and Theravada Buddhism have also attracted many followers. There are about a million Buddhists in the United States.

Left: The Samye Ling monastery in Scotland was the first Tibetan Buddhist center in Britain. It was founded in 1967.

Buddhism spreads

The map on the right shows how, over the last hundred years, Buddhism has spread outside Asia to North America, Europe, and Australia. The largest groups of Buddhists are in Europe and the United States.

NORTH AMERICA

EUROPE

ASIA

AFRICA

SOUTH AMERICA

Number of Buddhist centers in non-Buddhist countries.

AUSTRALIA

over 150

100–150

50–100

up to 50

Right: A Zen nun from the USA.

Western Buddhists

The Friends of the Western Buddhist Order was started in Britain in 1967 by Denis Lingwood. He was later ordained as a Buddhist monk, under the name Sangharaskshita. He wanted to form a Buddhist movement suited to Western society, which combined teachings and practices from Theravada, Tibetan, and Zen Buddhism.

Western art

From the 19th century onward, many writers and artists in Europe and the USA were inspired by Buddhism. Ideas and images from Buddhist art began to influence their work, such as this 19th-century French painting of the Buddha.

Left: Apart from monks and nuns, many ordinary people in the West have become Buddhists.

GLOSSARY

Avalokiteshvara: The most important bodhisattva in the Tibetan Buddhist religion. The Dalai Lama is believed to be the reincarnation of Avalokiteshvara.

Bodhi Tree: The sacred tree under which the Buddha attained enlightenment.

Bodhisattva: A perfect, heavenly being who has gained enlightenment but who delays entering nirvana in order to help other people.

Buddha: The Buddha is the spiritual name of the royal prince Siddhartha Gautauma, who became enlightened and then taught others, thus founding the Buddhist religion.

Confucianism: A religion based on the teaching of the Chinese philosopher Confucius who lived in China in the 6th and 5th centuries BCE.

Dharma: The Buddha's spiritual teachings.

Enlightenment: The spiritual state of true understanding, which all Buddhists would like to attain.

Five Precepts: Five promises that Buddhists make about how they will conduct their lives.

Four Noble Truths: Four truths that Buddhists must realize before they can achieve enlightenment.

Gandharan: A style of Buddhist art greatly influenced by the Greeks.

Gandharvas: Heavenly musicians who help to carry over a person's actions and their consequences between their death and their next rebirth.

Hinduism: A very ancient and diverse religion practiced on the Indian subcontinent.

Lama: The Tibetan word for a spiritual teacher or leader. The Dalai Lama is the greatest of these.

Lohan: A word in Chinese Buddhism for a person who has gained enlightenment, a "worthy one."

Mahayana: One of the two main schools of Buddhist thought (the other is called Theravada), practiced northwest of India (in Nepal, Tibet, China, Japan, Korea, and Vietnam).

Mandala: A circular picture representing the sacred world, used in Tibetan Buddhism for meditation.

Mantras: Powerful sacred sounds and words.

Meditation: The practice of fixing attention on one matter, having cleared the mind of all thoughts.

Mudra: A position of the hands in an image of the Buddha, which has a special meaning.

Nirvana: The state of enlightenment.

Noble Eightfold Path: Also called the Middle Path. A central concept of Buddhism that teaches people to avoid excess.

Pagoda: A temple built on several levels.

Prayer wheel: A metal cylinder with a small paper scroll inside on which thousands of prayers are written.

Puja: A ceremony of respect to the Buddha.

Pure Land: A school of Mahayana Buddhism developed in China. The Pure Land is a beautiful, peaceful place ruled by the bodhisattva Amitabha, to which Mahayana Buddhists aspire.

Sangha: The sangha is the name for all the Buddhist monk and nuns together.

Shinto: The ancient religion of Japan.

Silk Road: A series of trade routes across central Asia that linked the Mediterranean with India and China.

Stupa: A Buddhist monument which represents the Buddhist universe.

Sutras: In Mahayana Buddhism, a set of scriptures including teachings and stories of the Buddha and other monks. Sutra means "thread."

Tantras: A collection of mysterious sacred texts.

Tantric Buddhism: A type of Indian Buddhism that uses magic and rituals to help people achieve enlightenment.

Taoism: A religion based on the teaching of the Chinese philosopher Lao-tzu.

Theravada: One of the two main schools of Buddhist thought (the other is called Mahayana), practiced southeast of India (in Sri Lanka, Myanmar, Thailand, Cambodia, and Laos).

Three Jewels: The Buddha, the dharma, and the sangha together are known as the Three Jewels.

Vihara: A Buddhist monastery or temple.

Vinaya: The set of monastic rules in a Buddhist monastery.

Zen Buddhism: A school of Japanese Buddhism that was founded by the Indian monk Bodhidharma. The word Zen means "meditation."

INDEX

Amida 35
Amit'a-bul 35
Amitabha 28, 29, 35
Anagarika Dharmapala 42
Ananda 18
Ananda Maitreya 42
Ananda temple 33
Anarudhapura, Sri Lanka 25
Anathapindada 16
Angkor Wat 32
Aryans 11
Ashoka, Indian emperor 21, 24
Asia 9, 42, 43
Australia 43
Avalokiteshvara 29, 30, 31, 38, 39
Ayuthaya 33

Benares, India 10, 16
Bennet, Alan 42
Bhutan 26
Blavatsky, Helena 42
Bodh Gaya 13, 16, 36, 37
bodhi tree 13, 25, 36
Bodhidharma 34
Bon 38
Borododur 33
Brahma 31
Burma – see Myanmar
Buryat, Russia 41

Cambodia 19, 20, 21, 32
Central Asia 9, 28
Ceylon – see Sri Lanka
Channa 17
China 9, 19, 20, 22, 23, 27, 28, 29, 31, 34, 35, 38, 42
Christians 24
Colombo, Sri Lanka 25
Confucianism 28
Confucius 28

Daikoku 34
Dalai Lama 19, 39

dharma 8, 14, 16, 18, 29, 36, 37

Eight Requisites 18
Enma 35
Esoteric Buddhism 35
Europe 9, 43

Far East 21
Five Precepts 36, 42
Four Noble Truths 14

Gandharvas 30, 31
Ganesh 11
Gangarama Vihara monastery 25
Great Britain 42, 43
Great Vehicle – see Mahayana Buddhism
Guanyin 29, 30, 31

Himalayan mountains 10
Hinduism 9, 11, 32, 38
Hsuan Tang 28

India 8, 9, 11, 12, 14, 16, 18, 20, 21, 22, 23, 24, 26, 27, 36, 38, 39
Indonesia 32
Indra 12, 14
Indus Valley Civilization 11
Islam 32
Izu 35

Japan 18, 20, 21, 27, 34, 35, 36, 40, 42, 43
Jatakas 10
Java 33
Jizo 31
Jokharig temple 37

Kali 38
Kamakura, Japan 27
Kandy, Sri Lanka 40
Kanjur 22

Kannon 30
Kathina 41
King Suddhodana (the Buddha's father) 10
Korea 20, 21, 34, 35, 43
Ksitigarbha 31
Kukai 35
Kushinagara, India 16, 37
Kyoto, Japan 36

Lama 8
Laos 20, 32
Lao-tzu 28
Lhasa, Tibet 19, 37, 39
Lingwood, Denis 43
Lohan 29
London, England 42
Longmen, China 29
Losar 40
Lotus Sutra 22, 35
Lumbini 11, 37

Mahakasyapa 17
Mahaparinirvana 17
Mahayana Buddhism 18, 20, 22, 28, 29, 30, 38, 41
Mahinda 21
Maitreya 9
Malayasia 32
Mandalas 39
mantras 23
Mara 12, 13
meditation 12, 24, 36, 37
Mediterranean 9
Menandros – see Milinda
Middle Path 12, 14
Mikkyo Buddhism 35
Milinda, Greek king 20, 24
Mohenjo Daro 11
Mount Kailish 37
Mucalinda 13
Mudras 26
Muslims 24

Myanmar 20, 23, 32, 33

Nalanda monastery 28
Nepal 20
Nichiren Buddhism 35
nirvana 14, 15, 17, 28, 30, 38
Noble Eightfold Path 8, 14
North America 43
North Korea 34

O-bon 41
Olcott, Henry Steel 42

Padmasambhava 21, 38
Pagan, Myanmar 33
Pali Canon 22
Pali Text Society 42
Parakramabahu I, Sri Lankan
  king 24
Parilyyaka forest 14
parinirvana 25, 27
Parvati 11
Pilgrimage 37
Polonnaruwa, Sri Lanka 24, 25
Potala palace 19, 39
Prayer wheels 36
puja 37, 38
Pure Land 28, 29, 34, 35

Queen Maya (the Buddha's
  mother) 9

Rahula 18
Red Hats 39
Rhys Davids, Caroline 42
Rhys Davids, T.W. 42
Ritsu Buddhism 34

Russia 41

Sakya monastery 31
Samye Ling monastery 43
sangha 8, 18, 20, 24, 36
Sangharaskshita 43
Sarnath, India 14, 16, 24, 37
Scotland 43
Shakyamuni 10
Shakyas family 10
Shingon school of Buddhism 35
Shinkai 34
Shinto 34
Shiva 9, 11
Shotku, Korean prince 34
Siddhartha Gautama 8, 9, 10,
  11, 12, 13, 20, 28, 37
Silk Road 9, 21, 28
Singtsen Gampo, king 21
Sinhalese people 24, 25
Songsten Gamp, Tibetan king 38
Southeast Asia 27, 32, 33
South Korea 34
Soviet Union 41
Sravasti 16
Sri Lanka 18, 21, 24, 25, 27,
  32, 40, 41, 42
Stupas 17, 26, 27, 33
Sui Dynasty 28
Sutras 28

Tamils 24
Tantras 38
Tantric Buddhism 20, 38
Taoism 28
Tendai Buddhism 34, 36
Thailand 10, 18, 20, 21, 32, 33, 41

Theravada Buddhism 18, 20,
  22, 25, 32, 41, 42, 43
Three Baskets – see Pali Canon
Three Jewels 36, 38, 42
Tibet 9, 14, 15, 17, 18, 19, 20,
  21, 27, 31, 36, 37, 38, 39, 40
Tibetan Buddhism 43
Tibetan Buddhists 22, 23, 39
Tibetan festivals 40
Tipitaka – see Three Baskets
Tissa, Sri Lankan king 24, 25
Tusita Heaven 9

USA 9, 42, 43

Vajradhara 30
Vermont 42
Vietnam 20
Vishnu 32

Way of the Elders – see
  Theravada Buddhism
Wei T'o 30
Wesak 41
Western Paradise – see Pure
  Land
wheel of law 14
wheel of life 15
White Tara 30
World War II 34

Xuan-zang 23

Yama 15, 35
Yellow Hats 39

Zen Buddhism 34, 42, 43

Acknowledgements

The Publishers would like to thank the following photographers and picture libraries
for the photos used in this book.

t=top; tl=top left; tc=top center; tr=top right; c=center;
cl=center left; b=bottom; bl=bottom left; bc=bottom center; br=bottom right

Cover Marco Nardi/McRae Books Archives; **14t** Marco Nardi/McRae Books Archives; **18br** Index; **19bl** Index;
21bl Peter Charlesworth/JB Pictures/Grazia Neri; **25br** Werner Forman Archive/Index; **27tl, 27cr, 27cl, 27br**
Marco Nardi/McRae Books Archives; **27bl** Cosimo Bargellini; **29c** Werner Forman Archive/Index; **31tr** Index;
32 cl, 32b Marco Nardi/McRae Books Archives; **33tl** Marco Nardi/McRae Books Archives; **34br** Index;
36tl Index; **37tr** Index; **39bl** Werner Forman Archive/Index; **39br** Index; **40br** Misuru Kanamori/Arcadia Photo;
41tl, 41bl, 41br Hideo Haga/Arcadia Photo; **43t** Camerapress/Grazia Neri; **43bc** Jean-Marie Huron/Grazia Neri